TikTok Video Planner

This planner -- and all the creative video ideas herein -- belong to:

____

If found, please contact:

____

____

TikTok Video Planner

Grow Your Personal Brand and Have Fun on the Hottest New Social Media Platform

[Large Print Edition with
100 Video Creation Pages]

Created by:
Laura Petersen
@LaptopLaura

Title:
TikTok Video Planner: Grow Your Personal Brand and Have Fun on the Hottest New Social Media Platform

[Large Print Edition with 100 Video Creation Pages]

Printed: In the United States of America

First Edition: February 2020

Imprint: Copy That Pops

ISBN: 978-1-970111-06-4

Let's have fun with...

TikTok

Disclaimer:

The author and publisher do not claim to have ties to or endorsements from TikTok and/or TikTok's parent company.

This planner was created solely to help users of the application better organize their thoughts and ideas to make great videos.

What Is TikTok?

According to TikTok's website:
"*TikTok is the leading destination for short-form mobile video. Our mission is to inspire creativity and bring joy*."

What do they mean by "short-form video"?
60 seconds or less (often just 12 to 15 seconds).

How do they "inspire creativity and bring joy"?
Here are just a few of the things you can do, at the time of this writing, inside the TikTok app:
- overlay a huge selection of songs
- add visual effects before or after shooting
- save a draft (to finish and post later)
- turn on a countdown before filming starts
- create a "duet" with or "reaction" to another user (play your videos side-by-side)
- select a video cover (so you decide the short preview that others see)
- upload images to play as a slideshow
- and more!

A few stats:

• TikTok has over 500 million active users, behind only Whatsapp, Facebook, Facebook Messenger, WeChat, and Instagram (according to Datareportal, 2019)

• TikTok is 2nd most downloaded app in the world (as of early 2020)

PRO TIP:
Although TikTok's audience skews young, it won't be that way forever. Just as Facebook started as college-only and expanded, so too is TikTok's appeal and user base expanding to include a wider age demographic!

Long story, short:
It's worth having a presence on TikTok for business owners, personal brand builders, and anyone who wants to bring attention to what they care about.

Plus, it's super fun to be creative and produce your own version of trending video themes to match your personality, brand, lifestyle, and goals.

The Anatomy of a TikTok Video

As you scroll through your "Home" area inside your app, you are shown curated videos from people you are "Following" or selected by TikTok "For You."

You will see:
1. The video playing (shot vertically)
2. The handle (or user name) of the creator
3. When it was published
4. A short description (no more than 150 characters including hashtags)

5. The music used ("original sound" credited)
6. The profile photo of the account
7. How many likes the video has received
8. How many comments the video has received
9. A share button (to share with other users or to other platforms)
10. A spinning disc showing the album cover of the sound playing

The following two photos show:

Each of these 10 items above labeled -- on someone else's video vs. your own video.

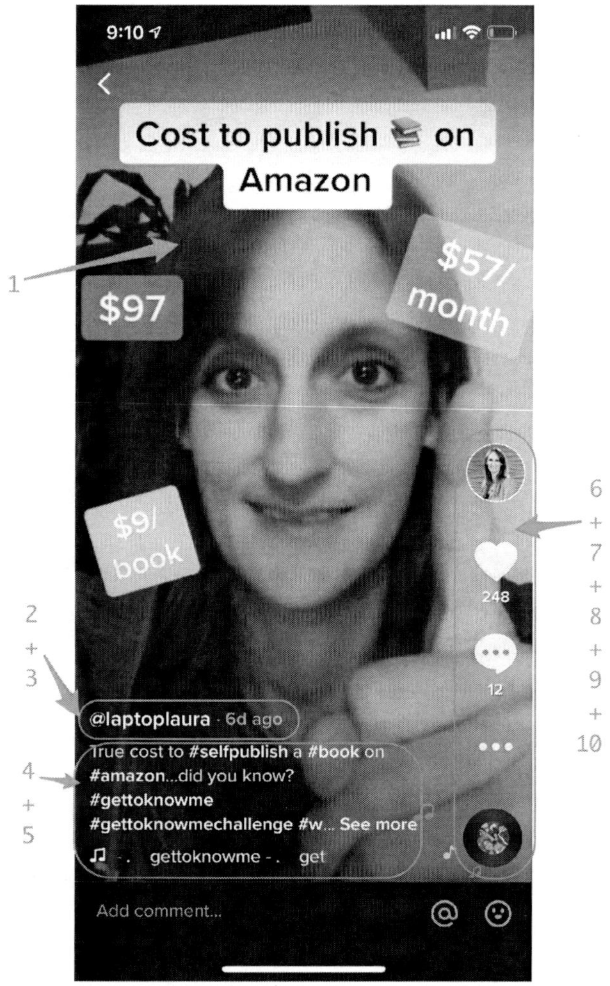

Who Is This Video Planner for?

This video planner is for anyone who wants to create educational, entertaining, or just plain fun videos on TikTok based on trending #tiktokchallenges or original ideas.

But…

You feel overwhelmed keeping track of things you need in your head, on notes apps in your phone, or random scraps of paper.

I often see a terrific video theme trending in the app and want to recreate it. But then I lose track of what music they used, what hashtags might help it be found, and what video segments I need to shoot to make it great.

Not anymore!

This TikTok video planner will help you to capture great video ideas and see them through to completion. You can even come back and notate how they performed!

The planner is great for kids, teens, tweens, and adults of all ages (whether you have a business yet or not). Its large print and ample doodle space make it easy to use and let your creativity flow!

I cannot wait to see what you create!

Please tag and share with me on TikTok. I'm @LaptopLaura.

xo
Laura

What's Inside?

In the following pages, you will find space to map out TikTok videos. Here are the steps to follow:

Step 1: Watch videos in your TikTok app that are currently trending or showing up in your "For You" page.

Step 2: When you see a video that catches your attention, makes you want to watch longer or a second time, and would be fun to create in your own way, jot down notes, ideas, hashtags, songs, and the video concept inside this planner.

Step 3: Map out a quick plan of what you need to shoot in order to create your own version -- and create your video!

Step 4: Post your video in TikTok!

Step 5: Share your video to other platforms and check back later to see how it performs!

Rinse + repeat!

On the next page, you will find a sample filled in.

Can't wait to see your videos going viral on TikTok!

Tag me on social media if you share! I'm @LaptopLaura on Facebook, Twitter, Instagram, and TikTok!

Okay, now get creatin'!

TikTok Video

____

Song: ______________________

Effects: ______________________

Concept: ______________________

____

____

____

Description + Hashtags:
(150 char)

____

____

____

____

____

Notes / Ideas / Examples:

ACTION ITEMS:

- ☐
- ☐
- ☐
- ☐
- ☐
- ☐

Posted date:

____

Performance Review / Reflection:

____

TikTok Video

____

Song:____________________________

Effects:__________________________

Concept:_________________________

____

____

____

Description + Hashtags:
(150 char)

____

____

____

____

____

Notes / Ideas / Examples:

ACTION ITEMS:

- [ ]
- [ ]
- [ ]
- [ ]
- [ ]
- [ ]

Posted date:

____

Performance Review / Reflection:

____

TikTok Video

____

Song:________________________

Effects:_______________________

Concept:______________________

____

____

____

Description + Hashtags:
(150 char)

____

____

____

____

____

Notes / Ideas / Examples:

ACTION ITEMS:

- [ ]
- [ ]
- [ ]
- [ ]
- [ ]
- [ ]

Posted date:

____

Performance Review / Reflection:

____

TikTok Video

VIDEO 1: Get to Know Me Challenge

Song: gettoknowme-

Effects: text on screen

Concept: Put up 'title' + 3 things not true -- swipe them off screen -- reveal truth

Description + Hashtags:
(150 char)

True cost to #selfpublish a #book on #Amazon...did you know?

#gettoknowme #writeabook
#gettoknowmechallenge
#storytime #writingabook

Notes / Ideas / Examples:

Cost to publish book on Amazon

$9/book
$57/month
$97 fee

NO! Free... they make $ only if you do

ACTION ITEMS:

- [x] shoot video
- [x] add text with "duration" (to reveal and hide as I swipe screen)
- [x] add copy/description
- [x] publish!
- [ ] ask 5 friends to like, comment, share

Posted date: 1/29/2020

Performance Review / Reflection: 31,500 views in 5 days! Do more like this!

TikTok Video

____

Song:______________________

Effects:______________________

Concept:______________________

____

____

____

Description + Hashtags:
(150 char)

____

____

____

____

____

Notes / Ideas / Examples:

ACTION ITEMS:

- [ ]
- [ ]
- [ ]
- [ ]
- [ ]
- [ ]

Posted date:

____

Performance Review / Reflection:

____

TikTok Video

Song:

Effects:

Concept:

Description + Hashtags:
(150 char)

Notes / Ideas / Examples:

ACTION ITEMS:

- ☐
- ☐
- ☐
- ☐
- ☐
- ☐

Posted date:

Performance Review / Reflection:

TikTok Video

Song:

Effects:

Concept:

Description + Hashtags:
(150 char)

Notes / Ideas / Examples:

ACTION ITEMS:

- [ ]
- [ ]
- [ ]
- [ ]
- [ ]
- [ ]

Posted date:

Performance Review / Reflection:

TikTok Video

Song:

Effects:

Concept:

Description + Hashtags:
(150 char)

Notes / Ideas / Examples:

ACTION ITEMS:

- ☐
- ☐
- ☐
- ☐
- ☐
- ☐

Posted date:

Performance Review / Reflection:

TikTok Video

____

Song:______________________

Effects:____________________

Concept:___________________

____

____

____

Description + Hashtags:
(150 char)

____

____

____

____

____

Notes / Ideas / Examples:

ACTION ITEMS:

- ☐
- ☐
- ☐
- ☐
- ☐
- ☐

Posted date:

____

Performance Review / Reflection:

____

TikTok Video

____

Song:______________________

Effects:______________________

Concept:______________________

____

____

____

Description + Hashtags:
(150 char)

____

____

____

____

____

Notes / Ideas / Examples:

ACTION ITEMS:

- [ ]
- [ ]
- [ ]
- [ ]
- [ ]
- [ ]

Posted date:

____

Performance Review / Reflection:

____

TikTok Video

____

Song:______________________

Effects:______________________

Concept:______________________

____

____

____

Description + Hashtags:
(150 char)

____

____

____

____

____

Notes / Ideas / Examples:

ACTION ITEMS:

- [ ]
- [ ]
- [ ]
- [ ]
- [ ]
- [ ]

Posted date: ______________

Performance Review / Reflection: ______________________

TikTok Video

____

Song: ______________________

Effects: ______________________

Concept: ______________________

____

____

____

Description + Hashtags:
(150 char)

____

____

____

____

____

Notes / Ideas / Examples:

ACTION ITEMS:

- ☐
- ☐
- ☐
- ☐
- ☐
- ☐

Posted date: ______________

Performance Review / Reflection: ______________________

TikTok Video

____

Song:______________________

Effects:______________________

Concept:____________________

____

____

____

Description + Hashtags:
(150 char)

____

____

____

____

____

Notes / Ideas / Examples:

ACTION ITEMS:

- ☐
- ☐
- ☐
- ☐
- ☐
- ☐

Posted date:

____

Performance Review / Reflection:

____

TikTok Video

Song:

Effects:

Concept:

Description + Hashtags:
(150 char)

Notes / Ideas / Examples:

ACTION ITEMS:

- [ ]
- [ ]
- [ ]
- [ ]
- [ ]
- [ ]

Posted date:

Performance Review / Reflection:

TikTok Video

____

Song: ____________________

Effects: ____________________

Concept: ____________________

____

____

____

Description + Hashtags:
(150 char)

____

____

____

____

____

Notes / Ideas / Examples:

ACTION ITEMS:

- [ ]
- [ ]
- [ ]
- [ ]
- [ ]
- [ ]

Posted date:

____

Performance Review / Reflection:

____

TikTok Video

____

Song:______________________

Effects:______________________

Concept:______________________

____

____

____

Description + Hashtags:
(150 char)

____

____

____

____

____

Notes / Ideas / Examples:

ACTION ITEMS:

- [ ]
- [ ]
- [ ]
- [ ]
- [ ]
- [ ]

Posted date:

____

Performance Review / Reflection:

____

TikTok Video

____

Song:________________________

Effects:________________________

Concept:________________________

____

____

____

Description + Hashtags:
(150 char)

____

____

____

____

____

Notes / Ideas / Examples:

ACTION ITEMS:

- ☐
- ☐
- ☐
- ☐
- ☐
- ☐

Posted date:

____

Performance Review / Reflection:

____

TikTok Video

Song:

Effects:

Concept:

Description + Hashtags:
(150 char)

Notes / Ideas / Examples:

ACTION ITEMS:

- [ ]
- [ ]
- [ ]
- [ ]
- [ ]
- [ ]

Posted date:

Performance Review / Reflection:

TikTok Video

Song:

Effects:

Concept:

Description + Hashtags:
(150 char)

Notes / Ideas / Examples:

ACTION ITEMS:

- [ ]
- [ ]
- [ ]
- [ ]
- [ ]
- [ ]

Posted date:

Performance Review / Reflection:

TikTok Video

____

Song:______________________

Effects:______________________

Concept:______________________

____

____

____

Description + Hashtags:
(150 char)

____

____

____

____

____

Notes / Ideas / Examples:

ACTION ITEMS:

- [ ]
- [ ]
- [ ]
- [ ]
- [ ]
- [ ]

Posted date:

____

Performance Review / Reflection:

____

TikTok Video

____

Song: ________________________

Effects: ________________________

Concept: ________________________

____

____

____

Description + Hashtags:
(150 char)

____

____

____

____

____

Notes / Ideas / Examples:

ACTION ITEMS:

- ☐
- ☐
- ☐
- ☐
- ☐
- ☐

Posted date: ____________

Performance Review / Reflection: ________________________

TikTok Video

____

Song:______________________

Effects:______________________

Concept:______________________

____

____

____

Description + Hashtags:
(150 char)

____

____

____

____

____

Notes / Ideas / Examples:

ACTION ITEMS:

- [ ]
- [ ]
- [ ]
- [ ]
- [ ]
- [ ]

Posted date:

____

Performance Review / Reflection:

____

TikTok Video

____

Song:______________________

Effects:____________________

Concept:___________________

____

____

____

Description + Hashtags:
(150 char)

____

____

____

____

____

Notes / Ideas / Examples:

ACTION ITEMS:

- [ ]
- [ ]
- [ ]
- [ ]
- [ ]
- [ ]

Posted date:

____

Performance Review / Reflection:

____

TikTok Video

____

Song: ____________________

Effects: ____________________

Concept: ____________________

____

____

____

Description + Hashtags:
(150 char)

____

____

____

____

____

Notes / Ideas / Examples:

ACTION ITEMS:

- [ ]
- [ ]
- [ ]
- [ ]
- [ ]
- [ ]

Posted date: ____________

Performance Review / Reflection: ____________________

TikTok Video

____

Song: ______________________

Effects: ______________________

Concept: ______________________

____

____

____

Description + Hashtags:
(150 char)

____

____

____

____

____

Notes / Ideas / Examples:

ACTION ITEMS:

- [ ]
- [ ]
- [ ]
- [ ]
- [ ]
- [ ]

Posted date:

____

Performance Review / Reflection:

____

TikTok Video

____

Song: ____________________

Effects: ____________________

Concept: ____________________

____

____

____

Description + Hashtags:
(150 char)

____

____

____

____

____

Notes / Ideas / Examples:

ACTION ITEMS:

- ☐
- ☐
- ☐
- ☐
- ☐
- ☐

Posted date: ____________

Performance Review / Reflection: ____________________

TikTok Video

____

Song: ______________________

Effects: ______________________

Concept: ______________________

____

____

____

Description + Hashtags:
(150 char)

____

____

____

____

____

Notes / Ideas / Examples:

ACTION ITEMS:

- [ ]
- [ ]
- [ ]
- [ ]
- [ ]
- [ ]

Posted date:

____

Performance Review / Reflection:

____

TikTok Video

____

Song:______________________

Effects:______________________

Concept:______________________

____

____

____

Description + Hashtags:
(150 char)

____

____

____

____

____

Notes / Ideas / Examples:

ACTION ITEMS:

- ☐
- ☐
- ☐
- ☐
- ☐
- ☐

Posted date:

____

Performance Review / Reflection:

____

TikTok Video

Song:

Effects:

Concept:

Description + Hashtags:
(150 char)

Notes / Ideas / Examples:

ACTION ITEMS:

- [ ]
- [ ]
- [ ]
- [ ]
- [ ]
- [ ]

Posted date:

Performance Review / Reflection:

TikTok Video

____

Song:______________________

Effects:______________________

Concept:______________________

____

____

____

Description + Hashtags:
(150 char)

____

____

____

____

____

Notes / Ideas / Examples:

ACTION ITEMS:

- [ ]
- [ ]
- [ ]
- [ ]
- [ ]
- [ ]

Posted date:

____

Performance Review / Reflection:

____

TikTok Video

____

Song: ______________________

Effects: ______________________

Concept: ______________________

____

____

____

Description + Hashtags:
(150 char)

____

____

____

____

____

Notes / Ideas / Examples:

ACTION ITEMS:

- [ ]
- [ ]
- [ ]
- [ ]
- [ ]
- [ ]

Posted date: ______________

Performance Review / Reflection: ______________________

TikTok Video

Song:

Effects:

Concept:

Description + Hashtags:
(150 char)

Notes / Ideas / Examples:

ACTION ITEMS:

- [ ]
- [ ]
- [ ]
- [ ]
- [ ]
- [ ]

Posted date:

Performance Review / Reflection:

TikTok Video

____

Song:____________________

Effects:____________________

Concept:____________________

____

____

____

Description + Hashtags:
(150 char)

____

____

____

____

____

Notes / Ideas / Examples:

ACTION ITEMS:

- [ ]
- [ ]
- [ ]
- [ ]
- [ ]
- [ ]

Posted date:

____

Performance Review / Reflection:

____

TikTok Video

Song:

Effects:

Concept:

Description + Hashtags:
(150 char)

Notes / Ideas / Examples:

ACTION ITEMS:

- [ ]
- [ ]
- [ ]
- [ ]
- [ ]
- [ ]

Posted date:

Performance Review / Reflection:

TikTok Video

Song:

Effects:

Concept:

Description + Hashtags:
(150 char)

Notes / Ideas / Examples:

ACTION ITEMS:

- [ ]
- [ ]
- [ ]
- [ ]
- [ ]
- [ ]

Posted date:

Performance Review / Reflection:

TikTok Video

____

Song: ______________________

Effects: ______________________

Concept: ______________________

____

____

____

Description + Hashtags:
(150 char)

____

____

____

____

____

Notes / Ideas / Examples:

ACTION ITEMS:

- [ ]
- [ ]
- [ ]
- [ ]
- [ ]
- [ ]

Posted date: ______________

Performance Review / Reflection: ______________________

TikTok Video

____

Song: ______________________

Effects: ______________________

Concept: ______________________

____

____

____

Description + Hashtags:
(150 char)

____

____

____

____

____

Notes / Ideas / Examples:

ACTION ITEMS:

- [ ]
- [ ]
- [ ]
- [ ]
- [ ]
- [ ]

Posted date:

____

Performance Review / Reflection:

____

TikTok Video

____

Song:______________________

Effects:____________________

Concept:___________________

____

____

____

Description + Hashtags:
(150 char)

____

____

____

____

____

Notes / Ideas / Examples:

ACTION ITEMS:

- [ ]
- [ ]
- [ ]
- [ ]
- [ ]
- [ ]

Posted date:

____

Performance Review / Reflection:

____

TikTok Video

____

Song: ______________

Effects: ______________

Concept: ______________

____

____

____

Description + Hashtags:
(150 char)

____

____

____

____

____

Notes / Ideas / Examples:

ACTION ITEMS:

- ☐
- ☐
- ☐
- ☐
- ☐
- ☐

Posted date: ______________

Performance Review / Reflection: ______________

TikTok Video

____

Song: ______________________

Effects: ______________________

Concept: ______________________

____

____

____

Description + Hashtags:
(150 char)

____

____

____

____

____

Notes / Ideas / Examples:

ACTION ITEMS:

- [ ]
- [ ]
- [ ]
- [ ]
- [ ]
- [ ]

Posted date: ______________

Performance Review / Reflection: ______________________

TikTok Video

____

Song: ____________________

Effects: ____________________

Concept: ____________________

____

____

____

Description + Hashtags:
(150 char)

____

____

____

____

____

Notes / Ideas / Examples:

ACTION ITEMS:

- ☐
- ☐
- ☐
- ☐
- ☐
- ☐

Posted date:

____

Performance Review / Reflection:

____

TikTok Video

____

Song:______________________

Effects:______________________

Concept:______________________

____

____

____

Description + Hashtags:
(150 char)

____

____

____

____

____

Notes / Ideas / Examples:

ACTION ITEMS:

- [ ]
- [ ]
- [ ]
- [ ]
- [ ]
- [ ]

Posted date:

____

Performance Review / Reflection:

____

TikTok Video

____

Song:______________________

Effects:______________________

Concept:______________________

____

____

____

Description + Hashtags:
(150 char)

____

____

____

____

____

Notes / Ideas / Examples:

ACTION ITEMS:

- [ ]
- [ ]
- [ ]
- [ ]
- [ ]
- [ ]

Posted date:

____

Performance Review / Reflection:

____

TikTok Video

____

Song: ______________________

Effects: ______________________

Concept: ______________________

____

____

____

Description + Hashtags:
(150 char)

____

____

____

____

____

Notes / Ideas / Examples:

ACTION ITEMS:

- [ ]
- [ ]
- [ ]
- [ ]
- [ ]
- [ ]

Posted date: ______________

Performance Review / Reflection: ______________________

TikTok Video

____

Song:______________________

Effects:______________________

Concept:______________________

____

____

____

Description + Hashtags:
(150 char)

____

____

____

____

____

Notes / Ideas / Examples:

ACTION ITEMS:

- ☐
- ☐
- ☐
- ☐
- ☐
- ☐

Posted date:

____

Performance Review / Reflection:

____

TikTok Video

____

Song:______________________

Effects:______________________

Concept:______________________

____

____

____

Description + Hashtags:
(150 char)

____

____

____

____

____

Notes / Ideas / Examples:

ACTION ITEMS:

- ☐
- ☐
- ☐
- ☐
- ☐
- ☐

Posted date: ______________

Performance Review / Reflection: ______________________

TikTok Video

____

Song: ______________________

Effects: ______________________

Concept: ______________________

____

____

____

Description + Hashtags:
(150 char)

____

____

____

____

____

Notes / Ideas / Examples:

ACTION ITEMS:

- ☐
- ☐
- ☐
- ☐
- ☐
- ☐

Posted date: ______________

Performance Review / Reflection: ______________________________

TikTok Video

____

Song: ______________________

Effects: ______________________

Concept: ______________________

____

____

____

Description + Hashtags:
(150 char)

____

____

____

____

____

Notes / Ideas / Examples:

ACTION ITEMS:

- [ ]
- [ ]
- [ ]
- [ ]
- [ ]
- [ ]

Posted date:

____

Performance Review / Reflection:

____

TikTok Video

Song:

Effects:

Concept:

Description + Hashtags:
(150 char)

Notes / Ideas / Examples:

ACTION ITEMS:

- [ ]
- [ ]
- [ ]
- [ ]
- [ ]
- [ ]

Posted date:

Performance Review / Reflection:

TikTok Video

____

Song: ______________________

Effects: ______________________

Concept: ______________________

____

____

____

Description + Hashtags:
(150 char)

____

____

____

____

____

Notes / Ideas / Examples:

ACTION ITEMS:

- [ ]
- [ ]
- [ ]
- [ ]
- [ ]
- [ ]

Posted date:

____

Performance Review / Reflection:

____

TikTok Video

____

Song:______________________

Effects:______________________

Concept:______________________

____

____

____

Description + Hashtags:
(150 char)

____

____

____

____

____

Notes / Ideas / Examples:

ACTION ITEMS:

- [ ]
- [ ]
- [ ]
- [ ]
- [ ]
- [ ]

Posted date:

____

Performance Review / Reflection:

____

TikTok Video

____

Song:______________________

Effects:______________________

Concept:______________________

____

____

____

Description + Hashtags:
(150 char)

____

____

____

____

____

Notes / Ideas / Examples:

ACTION ITEMS:

- ☐
- ☐
- ☐
- ☐
- ☐
- ☐

Posted date:

____

Performance Review / Reflection:

____

TikTok Video

____

Song: ______________________

Effects: ______________________

Concept: ______________________

____

____

____

Description + Hashtags:
(150 char)

____

____

____

____

____

Notes / Ideas / Examples:

ACTION ITEMS:

- ☐
- ☐
- ☐
- ☐
- ☐
- ☐

Posted date: ______________

Performance Review / Reflection: ______________________

TikTok Video

____

Song: ______________________

Effects: ______________________

Concept: ______________________

____

____

____

Description + Hashtags:
(150 char)

____

____

____

____

____

Notes / Ideas / Examples:

ACTION ITEMS:

- [ ]
- [ ]
- [ ]
- [ ]
- [ ]
- [ ]

Posted date: ______________

Performance Review / Reflection: ______________________

TikTok Video

____

Song: ______________________

Effects: ______________________

Concept: ______________________

____

____

____

Description + Hashtags:
(150 char)

____

____

____

____

____

Notes / Ideas / Examples:

ACTION ITEMS:

- [ ]
- [ ]
- [ ]
- [ ]
- [ ]
- [ ]

Posted date:

____

Performance Review / Reflection:

____

TikTok Video

____

Song:____________________

Effects:__________________

Concept:_________________

____

____

____

Description + Hashtags:
(150 char)

____

____

____

____

____

Notes / Ideas / Examples:

ACTION ITEMS:

☐ ☐

☐ ☐

☐ ☐

Posted date:

____

Performance Review / Reflection:

____

TikTok Video

____

Song: ______________________

Effects: ______________________

Concept: ______________________

____

____

____

Description + Hashtags:
(150 char)

____

____

____

____

____

Notes / Ideas / Examples:

ACTION ITEMS:

- [ ]
- [ ]
- [ ]
- [ ]
- [ ]
- [ ]

Posted date: ______________

Performance Review / Reflection: ______________________

TikTok Video

____

Song:______________________

Effects:______________________

Concept:______________________

____

____

____

Description + Hashtags:
(150 char)

____

____

____

____

____

Notes / Ideas / Examples:

ACTION ITEMS:

- [ ]
- [ ]
- [ ]
- [ ]
- [ ]
- [ ]

Posted date:

____

Performance Review / Reflection:

____

TikTok Video

____

Song: ______________________

Effects: ______________________

Concept: ______________________

____

____

____

Description + Hashtags:
(150 char)

____

____

____

____

____

Notes / Ideas / Examples:

ACTION ITEMS:

- [ ]
- [ ]
- [ ]
- [ ]
- [ ]
- [ ]

Posted date:

____

Performance Review / Reflection:

____

TikTok Video

____

Song:____________________________

Effects:____________________________

Concept:____________________________

____

____

____

Description + Hashtags:
(150 char)

____

____

____

____

____

Notes / Ideas / Examples:

ACTION ITEMS:

- ☐
- ☐
- ☐
- ☐
- ☐
- ☐

Posted date:

____

Performance Review / Reflection:

____

TikTok Video

____

Song:________________________

Effects:______________________

Concept:_____________________

____

____

____

Description + Hashtags:
(150 char)

____

____

____

____

____

Notes / Ideas / Examples:

ACTION ITEMS:

- [ ]
- [ ]
- [ ]
- [ ]
- [ ]
- [ ]

Posted date:

____

Performance Review / Reflection:

____

TikTok Video

____

Song:________________________

Effects:_______________________

Concept:______________________

____

____

____

Description + Hashtags:
(150 char)

____

____

____

____

____

Notes / Ideas / Examples:

ACTION ITEMS:

- ☐
- ☐
- ☐
- ☐
- ☐
- ☐

Posted date:

____

Performance Review / Reflection:

____

TikTok Video

____

Song: ____________________

Effects: ____________________

Concept: ____________________

____

____

____

Description + Hashtags:
(150 char)

____

____

____

____

____

Notes / Ideas / Examples:

ACTION ITEMS:

- [ ]
- [ ]
- [ ]
- [ ]
- [ ]
- [ ]

Posted date:

____

Performance Review / Reflection:

____

TikTok Video

____

Song: ______________________

Effects: ______________________

Concept: ______________________

____

____

____

Description + Hashtags:
(150 char)

____

____

____

____

____

Notes / Ideas / Examples:

ACTION ITEMS:

- [ ]
- [ ]
- [ ]
- [ ]
- [ ]
- [ ]

Posted date:

____

Performance Review / Reflection:

____

TikTok Video

____

Song: ____________

Effects: ____________

Concept: ____________

____

____

____

Description + Hashtags:
(150 char)

____

____

____

____

____

Notes / Ideas / Examples:

ACTION ITEMS:

- [ ]
- [ ]
- [ ]
- [ ]
- [ ]
- [ ]

Posted date: ____________

Performance Review / Reflection: ____________

TikTok Video

____

Song:______________________

Effects:______________________

Concept:______________________

____

____

____

Description + Hashtags:
(150 char)

____

____

____

____

____

Notes / Ideas / Examples:

ACTION ITEMS:

- [ ]
- [ ]
- [ ]
- [ ]
- [ ]
- [ ]

Posted date:

____

Performance Review / Reflection:

____

TikTok Video

____

Song: ______________________

Effects: ______________________

Concept: ______________________

____

____

____

Description + Hashtags:
(150 char)

____

____

____

____

____

Notes / Ideas / Examples:

ACTION ITEMS:

- ☐
- ☐
- ☐
- ☐
- ☐
- ☐

Posted date: ______________

Performance Review / Reflection: ______________________

TikTok Video

____

Song: ____________________

Effects: ____________________

Concept: ____________________

____

____

____

Description + Hashtags:
(150 char)

____

____

____

____

____

Notes / Ideas / Examples:

ACTION ITEMS:

- ☐
- ☐
- ☐
- ☐
- ☐
- ☐

Posted date:

____

Performance Review / Reflection:

____

TikTok Video

____

Song: ______________________________

Effects: ______________________________

Concept: ______________________________

____

____

____

Description + Hashtags:
(150 char)

____

____

____

____

____

Notes / Ideas / Examples:

ACTION ITEMS:

- [ ]
- [ ]
- [ ]
- [ ]
- [ ]
- [ ]

Posted date: ______________

Performance Review / Reflection: ______________________________

TikTok Video

____

Song: ____________________

Effects: ____________________

Concept: ____________________

____

____

____

Description + Hashtags:
(150 char)

____

____

____

____

____

Notes / Ideas / Examples:

ACTION ITEMS:

- [ ]
- [ ]
- [ ]
- [ ]
- [ ]
- [ ]

Posted date: ____________

Performance Review / Reflection: ____________________

TikTok Video

Song:

Effects:

Concept:

Description + Hashtags:
(150 char)

Notes / Ideas / Examples:

ACTION ITEMS:

- [ ]
- [ ]
- [ ]
- [ ]
- [ ]
- [ ]

Posted date:

Performance Review / Reflection:

TikTok Video

____

Song:______________________

Effects:______________________

Concept:______________________

____

____

____

Description + Hashtags:
(150 char)

____

____

____

____

____

Notes / Ideas / Examples:

ACTION ITEMS:

- ☐
- ☐
- ☐
- ☐
- ☐
- ☐

Posted date:

____

Performance Review / Reflection:

____

TikTok Video

____

Song: ____________

Effects: ____________

Concept: ____________

Description + Hashtags:
(150 char)

Notes / Ideas / Examples:

ACTION ITEMS:

- ☐
- ☐
- ☐
- ☐
- ☐
- ☐

Posted date:

Performance Review / Reflection:

TikTok Video

Song:

Effects:

Concept:

Description + Hashtags:
(150 char)

Notes / Ideas / Examples:

ACTION ITEMS:

- [ ]
- [ ]
- [ ]
- [ ]
- [ ]
- [ ]

Posted date:

Performance Review / Reflection:

TikTok Video

____

Song: ____________________

Effects: ____________________

Concept: ____________________

____

____

____

Description + Hashtags:
(150 char)

____

____

____

____

____

Notes / Ideas / Examples:

ACTION ITEMS:

- [ ]
- [ ]
- [ ]
- [ ]
- [ ]
- [ ]

Posted date:

____

Performance Review / Reflection:

____

TikTok Video

____

Song: ______________________

Effects: ______________________

Concept: ______________________

____

____

____

Description + Hashtags:
(150 char)

____

____

____

____

____

Notes / Ideas / Examples:

ACTION ITEMS:

- ☐
- ☐
- ☐
- ☐
- ☐
- ☐

Posted date: ______________

Performance Review / Reflection: ______________________

TikTok Video

Song:

Effects:

Concept:

Description + Hashtags:
(150 char)

Notes / Ideas / Examples:

ACTION ITEMS:

- [ ]
- [ ]
- [ ]
- [ ]
- [ ]
- [ ]

Posted date:

Performance Review / Reflection:

TikTok Video

____

Song: ______________________

Effects: ______________________

Concept: ______________________

____

____

____

Notes / Ideas / Examples:

Description + Hashtags:
(150 char)

____

____

____

____

____

ACTION ITEMS:

- [ ]
- [ ]
- [ ]
- [ ]
- [ ]
- [ ]

Posted date: ______________

Performance Review / Reflection: ______________________

TikTok Video

____

Song: ______________________

Effects: ______________________

Concept: ______________________

____

____

____

Description + Hashtags:
(150 char)

____

____

____

____

____

Notes / Ideas / Examples:

ACTION ITEMS:

- [ ]
- [ ]
- [ ]
- [ ]
- [ ]
- [ ]

Posted date: ______________

Performance Review / Reflection: ______________________

TikTok Video

Song:

Effects:

Concept:

Description + Hashtags:
(150 char)

Notes / Ideas / Examples:

ACTION ITEMS:

- [ ]
- [ ]
- [ ]
- [ ]
- [ ]
- [ ]

Posted date:

Performance Review / Reflection:

TikTok Video

____

Song:______________________

Effects:______________________

Concept:______________________

____

____

____

Description + Hashtags:
(150 char)

____

____

____

____

____

Notes / Ideas / Examples:

ACTION ITEMS:

- [ ]
- [ ]
- [ ]
- [ ]
- [ ]
- [ ]

Posted date:

____

Performance Review / Reflection:

____

TikTok Video

____

Song: ______________________

Effects: ______________________

Concept: ______________________

____

____

____

Description + Hashtags:
(150 char)

____

____

____

____

____

Notes / Ideas / Examples:

ACTION ITEMS:

- ☐
- ☐
- ☐
- ☐
- ☐
- ☐

Posted date:

____

Performance Review / Reflection:

____

TikTok Video

____

Song:______________________

Effects:______________________

Concept:____________________

____

____

____

Description + Hashtags:
(150 char)

____

____

____

____

____

Notes / Ideas / Examples:

ACTION ITEMS:

- ☐
- ☐
- ☐
- ☐
- ☐
- ☐

Posted date:

____

Performance Review / Reflection:

____

TikTok Video

____

Song: ____________________

Effects: ____________________

Concept: ____________________

____

____

____

Description + Hashtags:
(150 char)

____

____

____

____

____

Notes / Ideas / Examples:

ACTION ITEMS:

- [ ]
- [ ]
- [ ]
- [ ]
- [ ]
- [ ]

Posted date: ____________

Performance Review / Reflection: ____________________

TikTok Video

____

Song: ____________________

Effects: ____________________

Concept: ____________________

____

____

____

Description + Hashtags:
(150 char)

____

____

____

____

____

Notes / Ideas / Examples:

ACTION ITEMS:

- [ ]
- [ ]
- [ ]
- [ ]
- [ ]
- [ ]

Posted date:

____

Performance Review / Reflection:

____

TikTok Video

____

Song: ______________________

Effects: ______________________

Concept: ______________________

____

____

____

Description + Hashtags:
(150 char)

____

____

____

____

____

Notes / Ideas / Examples:

ACTION ITEMS:

- [ ]
- [ ]
- [ ]
- [ ]
- [ ]
- [ ]

Posted date: ______________

Performance Review / Reflection: ______________________

TikTok Video

____

Song: ______________________

Effects: ______________________

Concept: ______________________

____

____

____

Description + Hashtags:
(150 char)

____

____

____

____

____

Notes / Ideas / Examples:

ACTION ITEMS:

- ☐
- ☐
- ☐
- ☐
- ☐
- ☐

Posted date: ______________

Performance Review / Reflection: ______________________

TikTok Video

____

Song: ____________

Effects: ____________

Concept: ____________

____

____

____

Description + Hashtags:
(150 char)

____

____

____

____

____

Notes / Ideas / Examples:

ACTION ITEMS:

- [ ]
- [ ]
- [ ]
- [ ]
- [ ]
- [ ]

Posted date: ____________

Performance Review / Reflection: ____________

TikTok Video

____

Song:____________________

Effects:____________________

Concept:____________________

____

____

____

Description + Hashtags:
(150 char)

____

____

____

____

____

Notes / Ideas / Examples:

ACTION ITEMS:

- ☐
- ☐
- ☐
- ☐
- ☐
- ☐

Posted date:

____

Performance Review / Reflection:

____

TikTok Video

____

Song: ______________________

Effects: ______________________

Concept: ______________________

____

____

____

Description + Hashtags:
(150 char)

____

____

____

____

____

Notes / Ideas / Examples:

ACTION ITEMS:

- [ ]
- [ ]
- [ ]
- [ ]
- [ ]
- [ ]

Posted date:

____

Performance Review / Reflection:

____

TikTok Video

____

Song: ______________________

Effects: ______________________

Concept: ______________________

____

____

____

Description + Hashtags:
(150 char)

____

____

____

____

____

Notes / Ideas / Examples:

ACTION ITEMS:

- [ ]
- [ ]
- [ ]
- [ ]
- [ ]
- [ ]

Posted date:

____

Performance Review / Reflection:

____

TikTok Video

Song:

Effects:

Concept:

Description + Hashtags:
(150 char)

Notes / Ideas / Examples:

ACTION ITEMS:

- [ ]
- [ ]
- [ ]
- [ ]
- [ ]
- [ ]

Posted date:

Performance Review / Reflection:

TikTok Video

____

Song: ______________

Effects: ______________

Concept: ______________

____

____

____

Description + Hashtags:
(150 char)

____

____

____

____

____

Notes / Ideas / Examples:

ACTION ITEMS:

- ☐
- ☐
- ☐
- ☐
- ☐
- ☐

Posted date: ______________

Performance Review / Reflection: ______________

TikTok Video

____

Song: ____________________

Effects: ____________________

Concept: ____________________

____

____

____

Description + Hashtags:
(150 char)

____

____

____

____

____

Notes / Ideas / Examples:

ACTION ITEMS:

- [ ]
- [ ]
- [ ]
- [ ]
- [ ]
- [ ]

Posted date: ____________

Performance Review / Reflection: ____________________

TikTok Video

____

Song: ____________________

Effects: ____________________

Concept: ____________________

____

____

____

Description + Hashtags:
(150 char)

____

____

____

____

____

Notes / Ideas / Examples:

ACTION ITEMS:

- [ ]
- [ ]
- [ ]
- [ ]
- [ ]
- [ ]

Posted date:

____

Performance Review / Reflection:

____

TikTok Video

____

Song: ____________________

Effects: ____________________

Concept: ____________________

____

____

____

Description + Hashtags:
(150 char)

____

____

____

____

____

Notes / Ideas / Examples:

ACTION ITEMS:

- [ ]
- [ ]
- [ ]
- [ ]
- [ ]
- [ ]

Posted date:

____

Performance Review / Reflection:

____

TikTok Video

____

Song: ______________________

Effects: ______________________

Concept: ______________________

____

____

____

Description + Hashtags:
(150 char)

____

____

____

____

____

Notes / Ideas / Examples:

ACTION ITEMS:

- [ ]
- [ ]
- [ ]
- [ ]
- [ ]
- [ ]

Posted date: ______________

Performance Review / Reflection: ______________________

TikTok Video

Song:

Effects:

Concept:

Description + Hashtags:
(150 char)

Notes / Ideas / Examples:

ACTION ITEMS:

- [ ]
- [ ]
- [ ]
- [ ]
- [ ]
- [ ]

Posted date:

Performance Review / Reflection:

TikTok Video

____

Song:______________________

Effects:______________________

Concept:______________________

____

____

____

Description + Hashtags:
(150 char)

____

____

____

____

____

Notes / Ideas / Examples:

ACTION ITEMS:

- [ ]
- [ ]
- [ ]
- [ ]
- [ ]
- [ ]

Posted date:

____

Performance Review / Reflection:

____

TikTok Video

____

Song: ____________________

Effects: ____________________

Concept: ____________________

____

____

____

Notes / Ideas / Examples:

Description + Hashtags:
(150 char)

____

____

____

____

____

ACTION ITEMS:

- [ ]
- [ ]
- [ ]
- [ ]
- [ ]
- [ ]

Posted date: ____________

Performance Review / Reflection: ____________________

TikTok Video

____

Song:______________________

Effects:______________________

Concept:______________________

____

____

____

Description + Hashtags:
(150 char)

____

____

____

____

____

Notes / Ideas / Examples:

ACTION ITEMS:

- [ ]
- [ ]
- [ ]
- [ ]
- [ ]
- [ ]

Posted date:

____

Performance Review / Reflection:

____

TikTok

Happy Creating!

Make sure to tag me on videos
that you make using this planner.

I will be so happy to like, comment
on, and share them! 😀

@LaptopLaura

To learn more about Laura Petersen, visit
LaptopLaura.com and CopyThatPops.com.

Made in United States
Cleveland, OH
05 November 2026

47662561R00063